GREAT PIANO SOLOS

GREAT PIANO SOLOS

Wise Publications
London/New York/Paris/Sydney/Copenhagen/Berlin/Madrid/Tokyo

Exclusive Distributors:
Music Sales Limited
8/9 Frith Street,
London W1V 5TZ, England.
Music Sales Pty Limited
120 Rothschild Avenue,
Rosebery, NSW 2018,
Australia.

Order No. AM970167
ISBN 0-7119-8816-1
This book © Copyright 2002 by Wise Publications.
www.musicsales.com

Printed in Malta by Interprint Limited.

Your Guarantee of Quality:
As publishers, we strive to produce every book to the highest commercial
standards. This book has been carefully designed to minimise awkward
page turns and to make playing from it a real pleasure. Particular care has
been given to specifying acid-free, neutral-sized paper made from pulps
which have not been elemental chlorine bleached. This pulp is from farmed
sustainable forests and was produced with special regard for the
environment. Throughout, the printing and binding have been planned to
ensure a sturdy, attractive publication which should give years of
enjoyment. If your copy fails to meet our high standards, please inform us
and we will gladly replace it.

CONTENTS

Adagio For Strings, Op.11

By Samuel Barber

Moderato adagio (very slowly)

(with increasing intensity)

Air On The G String
(from "Suite No. 3 in D")

By Johann Sebastian Bach

Lento, poco rubato (♩ = c.48)

Molto rall.

Clair de Lune
(from "Suite Bergamasque")

By Claude Debussy

morendo jusqu'à la fin

Für Elise

By Ludwig Van Beethoven

Poco moto

Morning
(from "Peer Gynt")

By Edvard Grieg

Moderately fast

Prelude in E Minor, Op.28 No.4

By Frederic Chopin

Pie Jesu
(from "Requiem, Op. 48")

By Gabriel Fauré

27

Rondo Alla Turca
(from "Piano Sonata No.11 in A Major")

By Wolfgang Amadeus Mozart

Allegretto

29

American Beauty / Angela Undress
(from "American Beauty")

By Thomas Newman

I. MAIN THEME

II. ANGELA UNDRESS

Cavatina
(from "The Deer Hunter")

By Stanley Myers

39

Crouching Tiger, Hidden Dragon / Eternal Vow
(from "Crouching Tiger, Hidden Dragon")

By Tan Dun

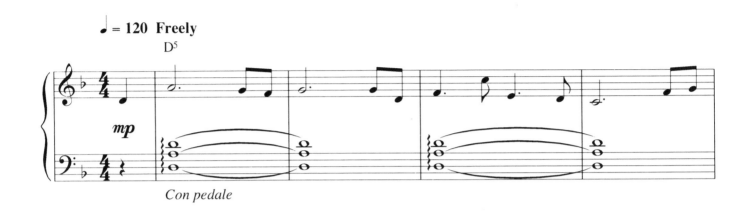

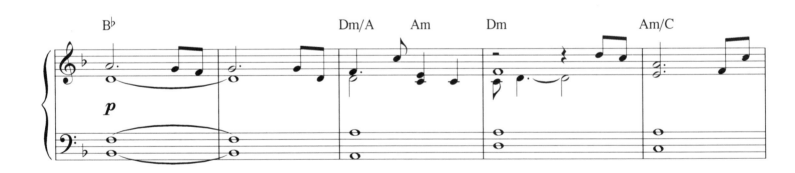

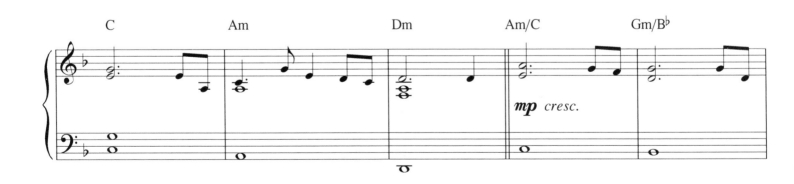

Feather Theme
(Main Title from the film "Forrest Gump")

By Alan Silvestri

For The Love Of A Princess
(from "Braveheart")

By James Horner

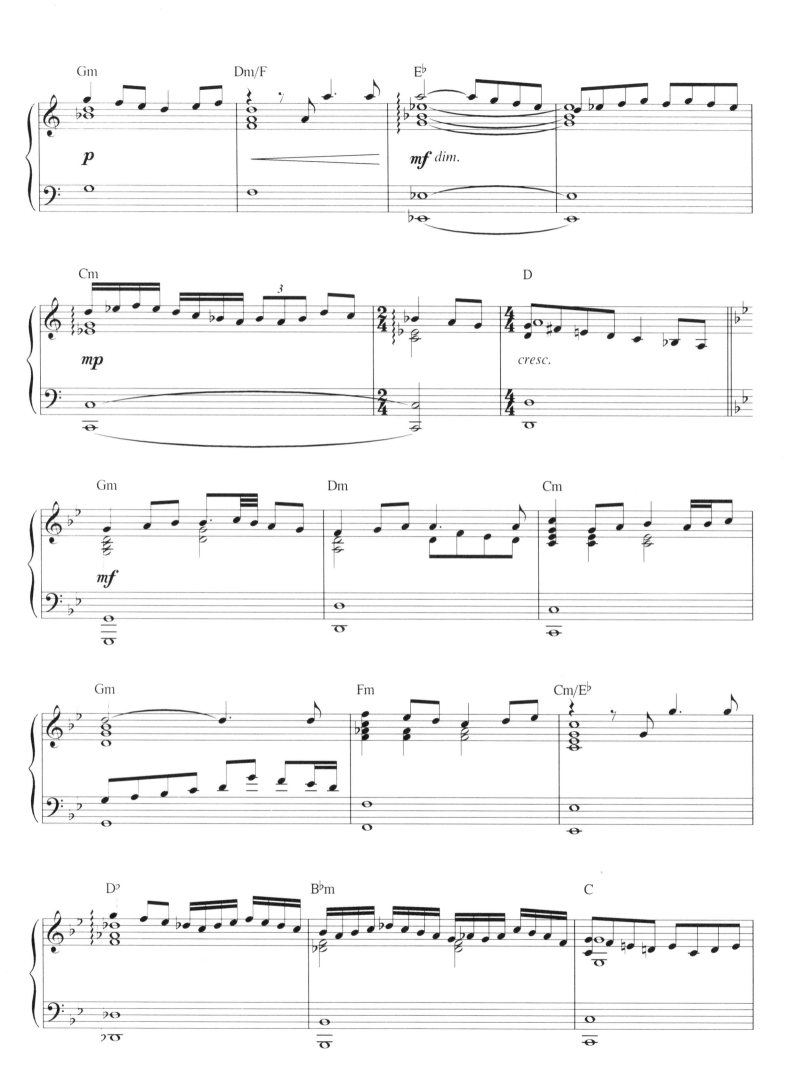

Lara's Theme
(from "Doctor Zhivago")

By Maurice Jarre

T043819

Raiders March
(from "Raiders Of The Lost Ark")

By John Williams

54

The Beginning Of The Partnership
(from the film "Shakespeare In Love")

By Stephen Warbeck

All I Have To Do Is Dream

Words & Music by Boudleaux Bryant

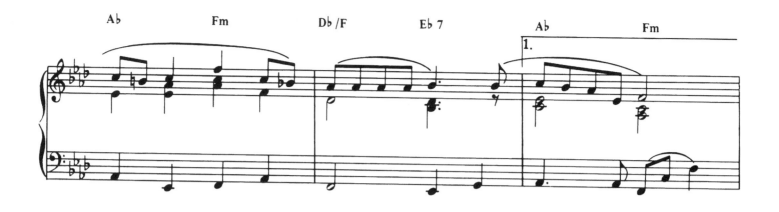

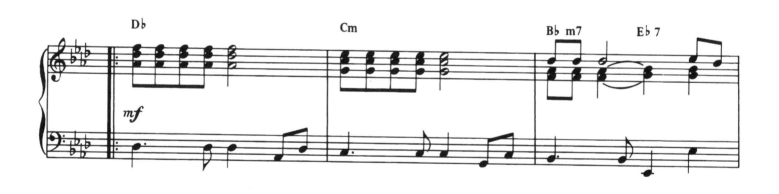

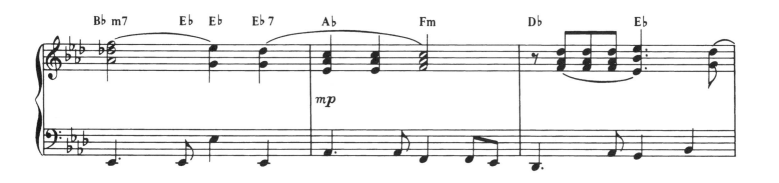

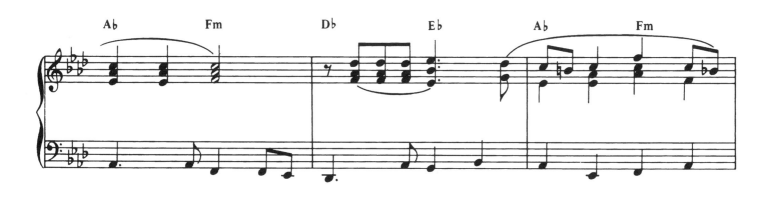

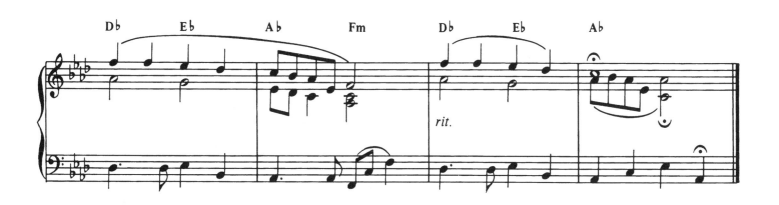

My Way

Original Words & Music by Claude Francois, Jacques Revaux & Gilles Thibaut
English Words by Paul Anka

63

Can't Help Falling In Love

Words & Music by George David Weiss, Hugo Peretti & Luigi Creatore

D7(9♭)   Gm   Fm7   B♭7

E♭   Gm   Cm   Cm/B♭   A♭   E♭

1
B♭   A♭   G   Cm   B♭7

2
Cm   B♭7   E   B♭7   E♭   B♭7

E♭   B♭7   C7   tacet _ _ _ _ _ _ _ * E♭   B♭7

E♭   B♭7   E♭   B♭7   E♭

Somethin' Stupid

Words & Music by C. Carson Parks

68

69

Stardust

Words by Mitchell Parish
Music by Hoagy Carmichael

Em7

C9(11+)

(ped. sim.)

Gm

D⁶₉

F♯m

B9

Em7

B9

G6

Gm

D F♯m Bm7 D

8ᵛᵃ

sfz

C♯7

F♯7

Em7

B7 Bdim

A7

D6

8ᵛᵃ

8ᵛᵃ

loco

sfz

sfz

C9

D⁶₉

When I Fall In Love

Music by Victor Young
Words by Edward Heyman

What The World Needs Now Is Love

Words by Hal David
Music by Burt Bacharach

F#m

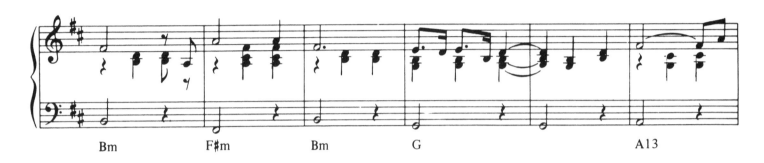

Bm   F#m   Bm   G   A13

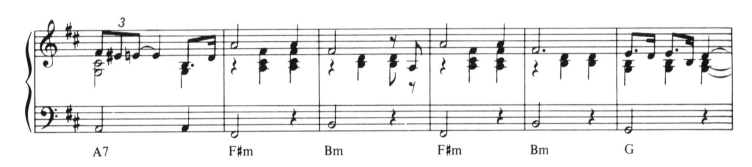

A7   F#m   Bm   F#m   Bm   G

F#11   F#7   F#m/B

Am7   D7   Gmaj7   G6

77

Unchained Melody

Words by Hy Zaret
Music by Alex North

Moderately slow

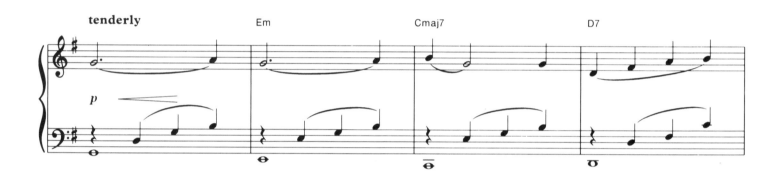

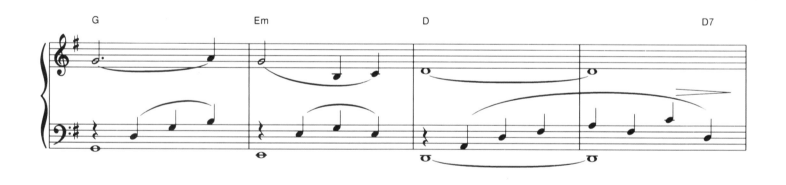

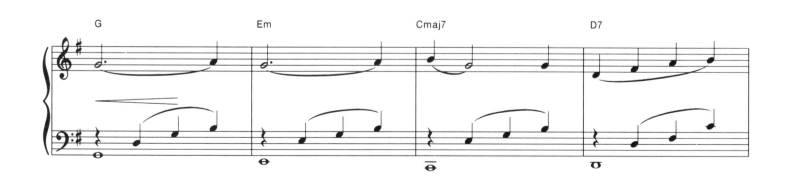

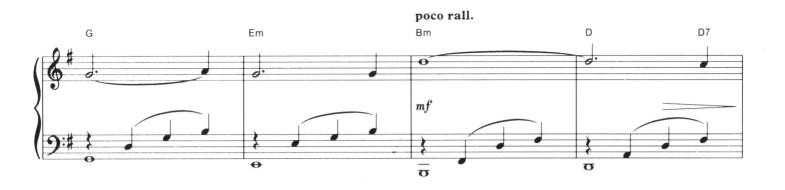

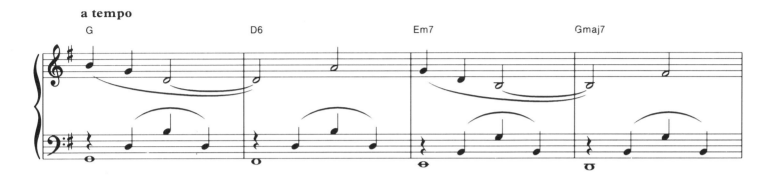

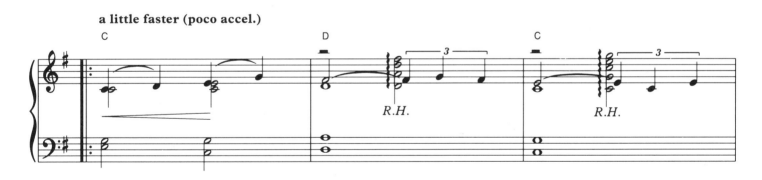

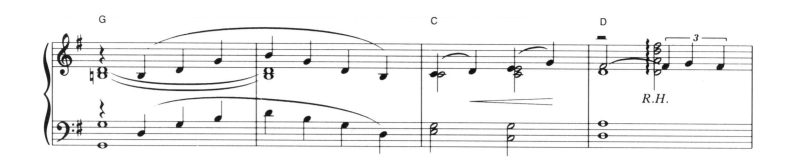

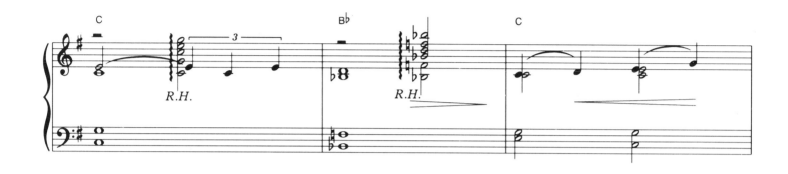

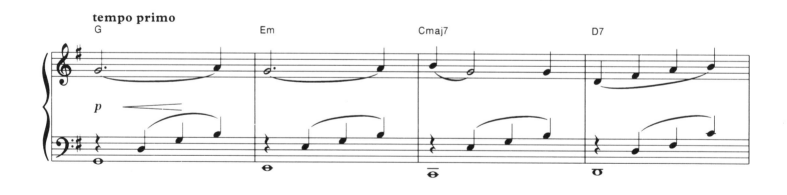

tempo primo

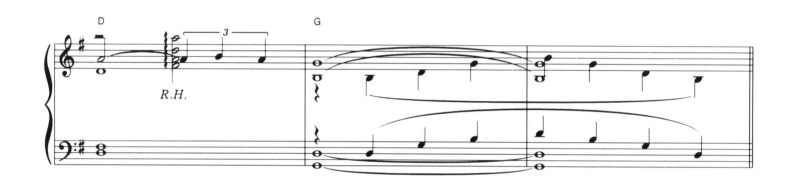

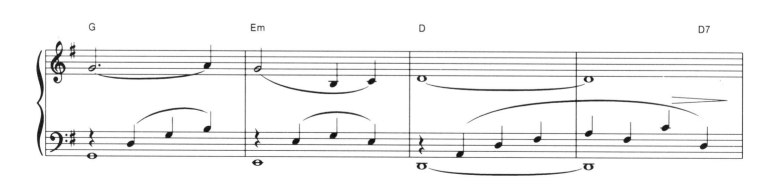

Ain't Misbehavin'

Words by Andy Razaf
Music by Thomas 'Fats' Waller & Harry Brooks

84

86

The Entertainer

By Scott Joplin

89

I Wish I Knew How It Would Feel To Be Free

Words by Billy Taylor & Dick Dallas
Music by Billy Taylor

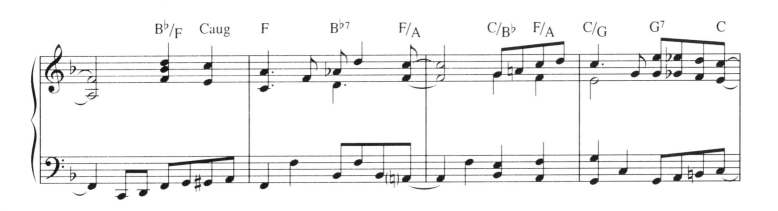

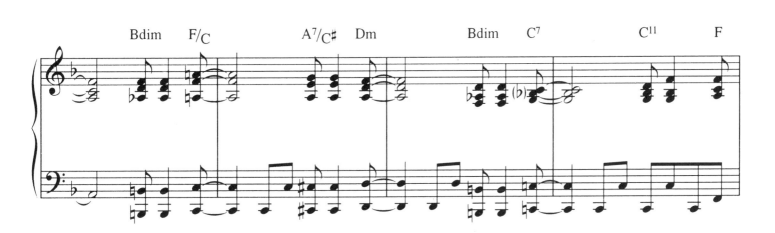

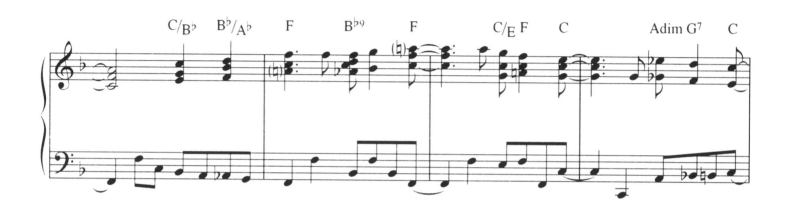

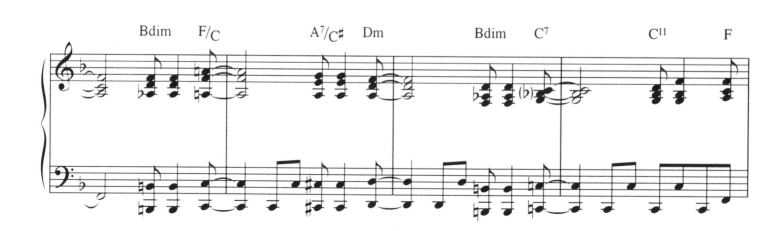

Moonlight Serenade

Words by Mitchell Parish
Music by Glenn Miller

My Baby Just Cares For Me

Words by Gus Kahn
Music by Walter Donaldson

99

God Bless' The Child

Words & Music by Arthur Herzog Jr. & Billie Holiday

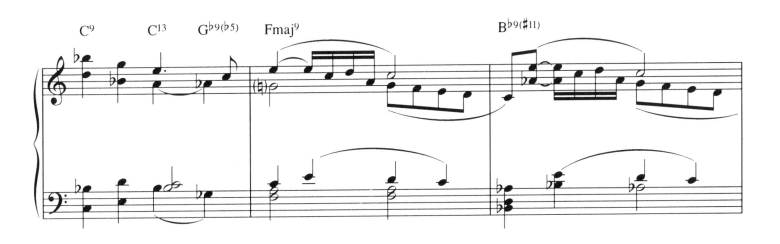

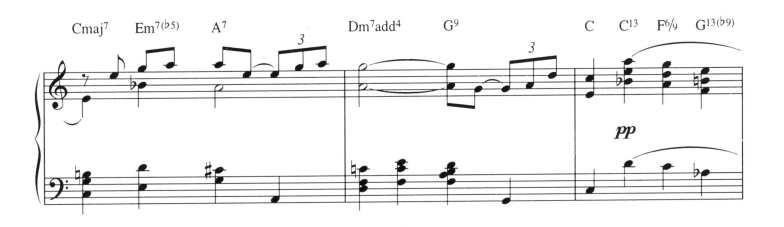

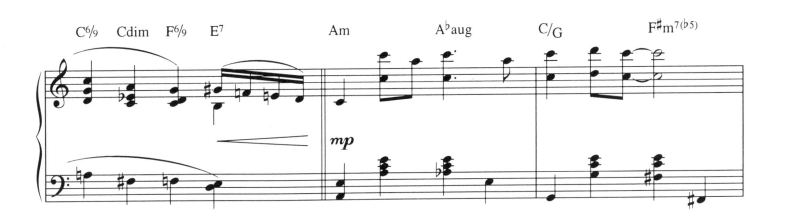

Solitude

Words by Eddie de Lange & Irving Mills
Music by Duke Ellington

Moderately

a tempo

Dbmaj7   Fm7 Db13 Gb6   B9(b5)   Ebm7/Ab

D   Dbmaj7 Bb7(b9) Eb9   Ab13   Dbmaj7

Fm7 Bbm7   Ebm7   Eb9   Ebm7/Ab Fm   Ebm7/Ab Ab7 D7

Dbmaj7   Gb6   Gdim

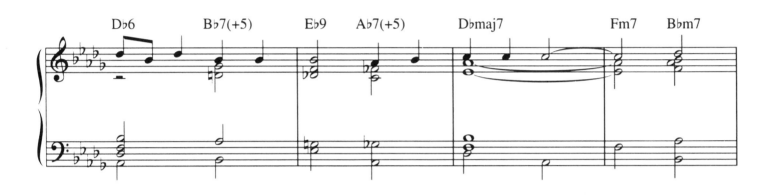

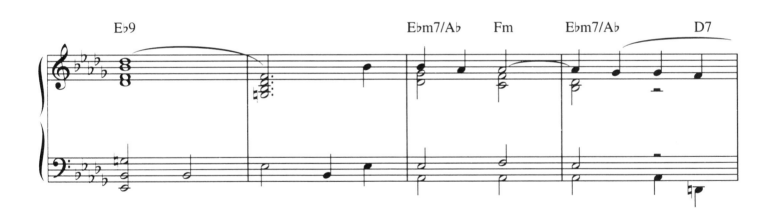

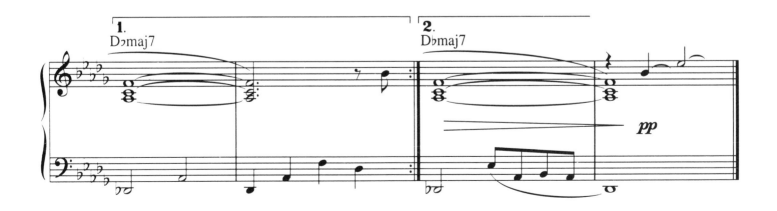

Eternity

Words & Music by Robbie Williams & Guy Chambers

Fields Of Gold

Words & Music by Sting

Flowing moderately

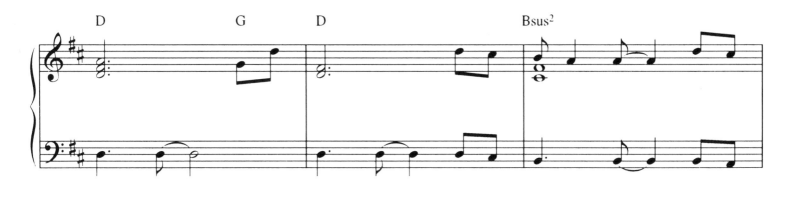

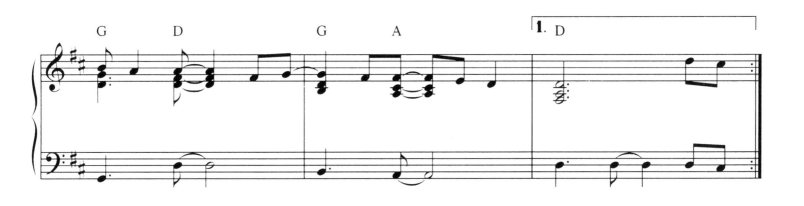

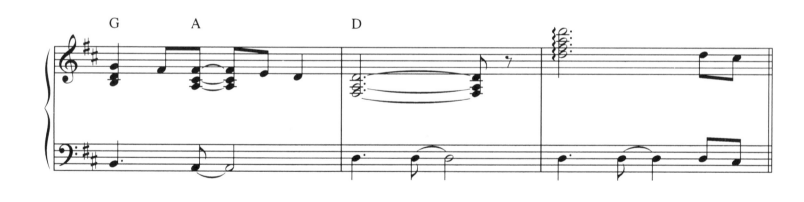

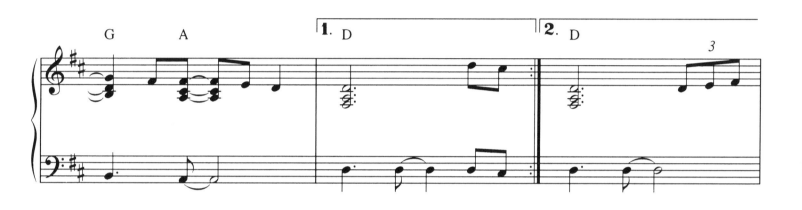

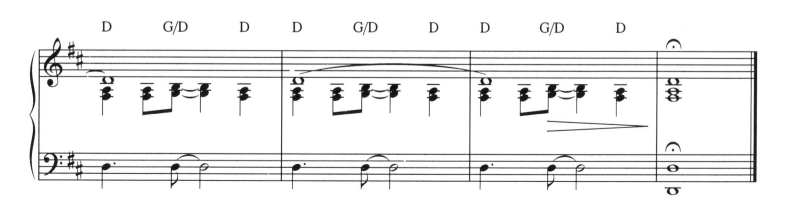

Have I Told You Lately

Words & Music by Van Morrison

119

Time To Say Goodbye (Con Te Partirò)

Words & Music by Lucio Quarantotto & Francesco Sartori
Adapted by Frank Peterson

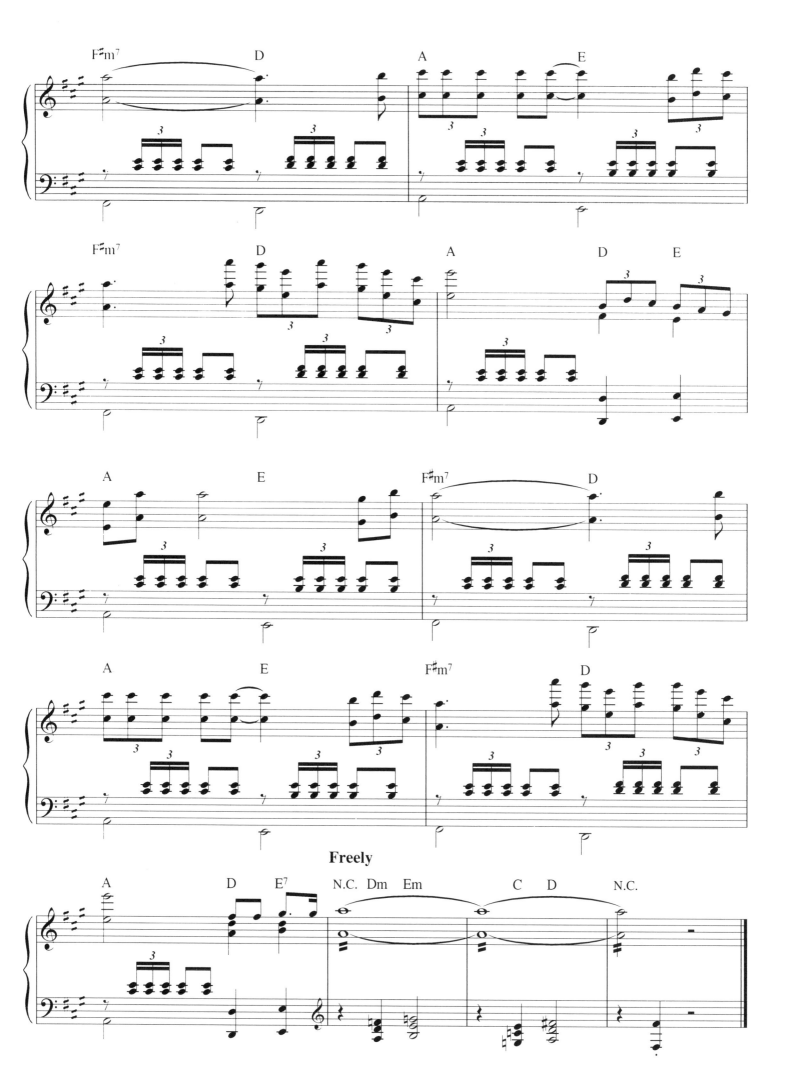

123

Trouble

Words & Music by Guy Berryman, Jon Buckland, Will Champion & Chris Martin

Evergreen

Words & Music by Jörgen Elofsson, Per Magnusson & David Kreuger

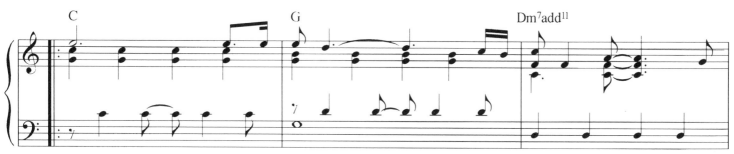

128

Your Song

Words & Music by Elton John & Bernie Taupin

Slow, but with a beat

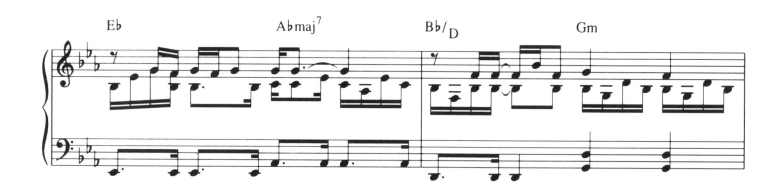

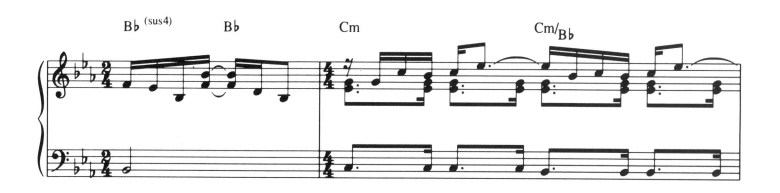

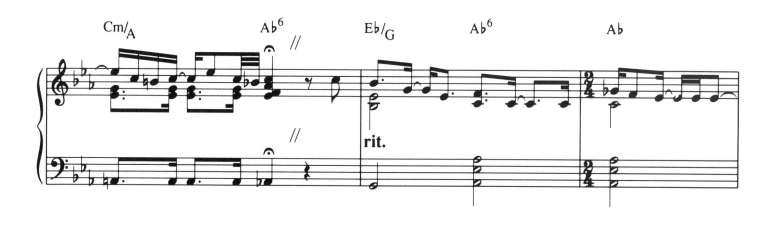

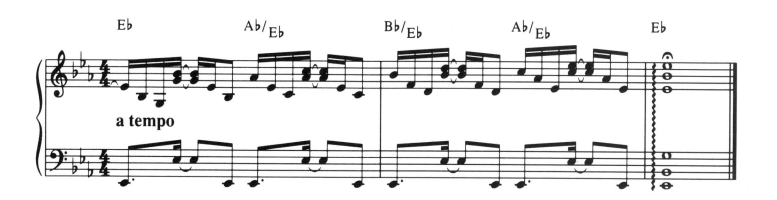

Close Every Door

(from "Joseph And The Amazing Technicolor Dreamcoat")

Words by Tim Rice
Music by Andrew Lloyd Webber

137

Is You Is Or Is You Ain't My Baby?

(from "Five Guys Named Moe")

Words & Music by Billy Austin & Louis Jordan

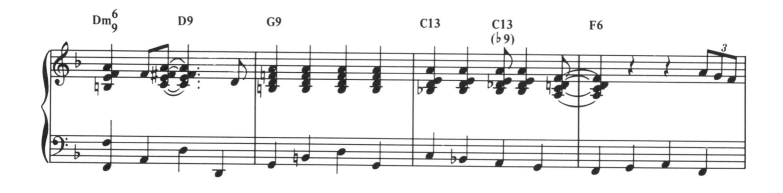

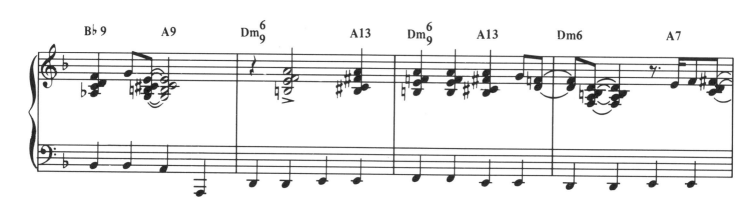

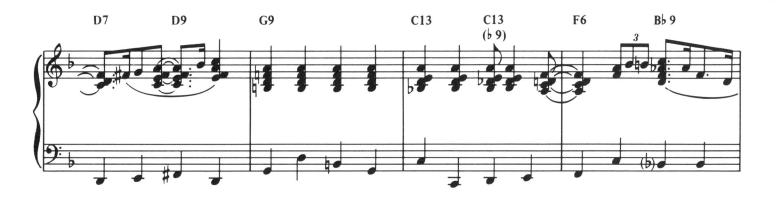

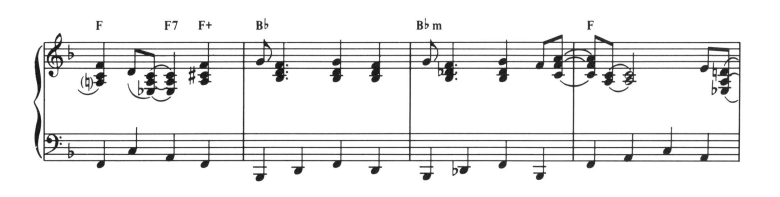

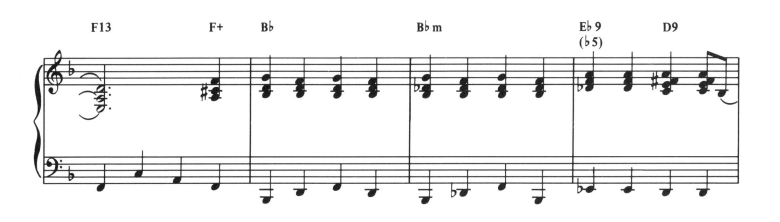

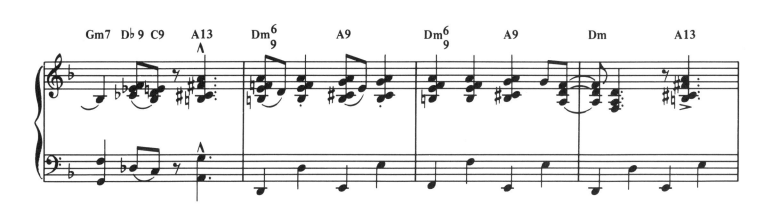

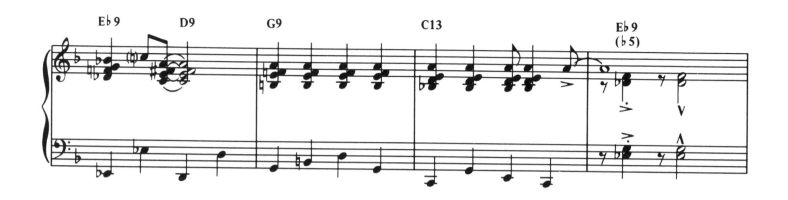

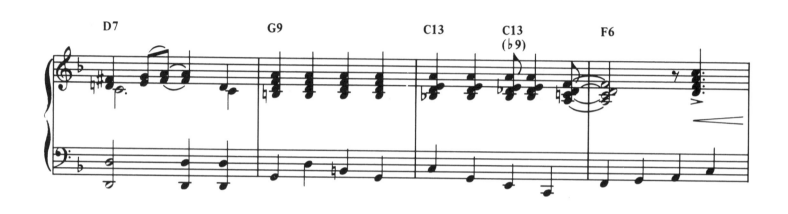

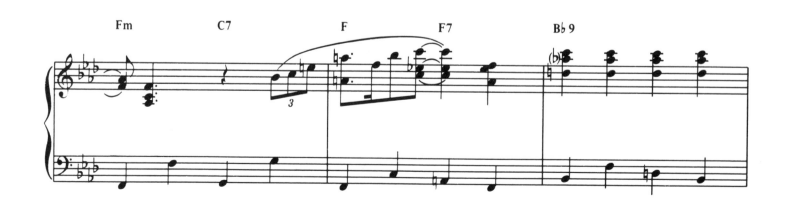

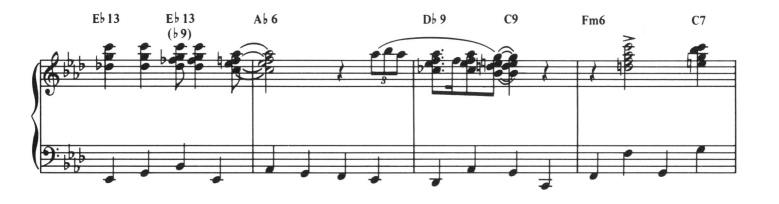

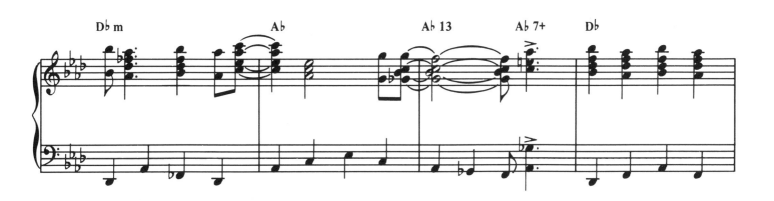

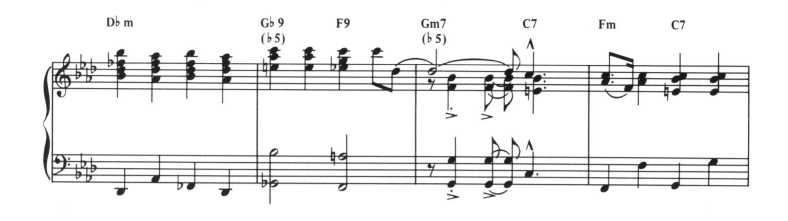

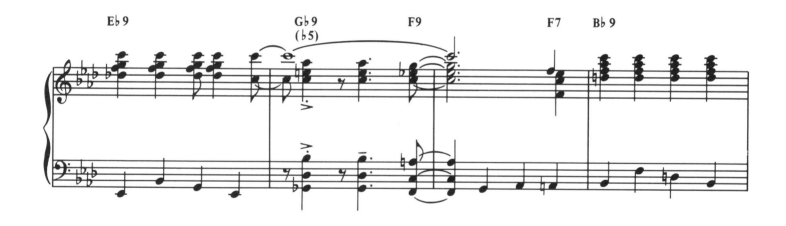

Memory

(from "Cats")

Music by Andrew Lloyd Webber
Lyrics by Trevor Nunn after T.S. Eliot

On My Own
(from "Les Misérables")

Music by Claude-Michel Schönberg
Lyrics by Alain Boublil, Jean-Marc Natel, Herbert Kretzmer, Trevor Nunn & John Caird

Somewhere

(from "West Side Story")

Words by Stephen Sondheim
Music by Leonard Bernstein

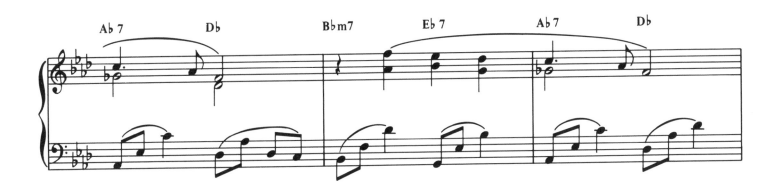

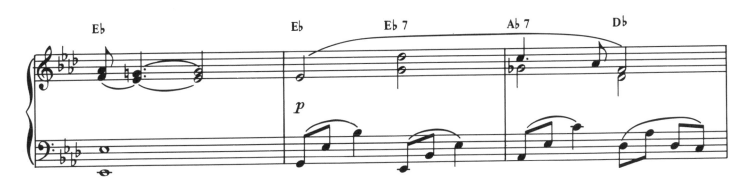

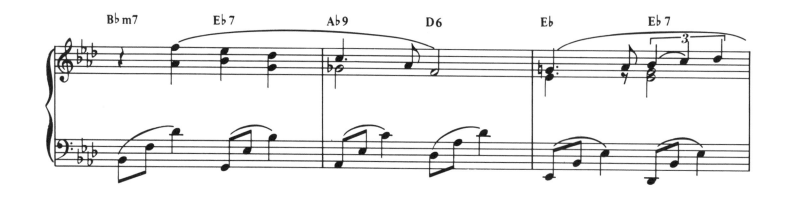

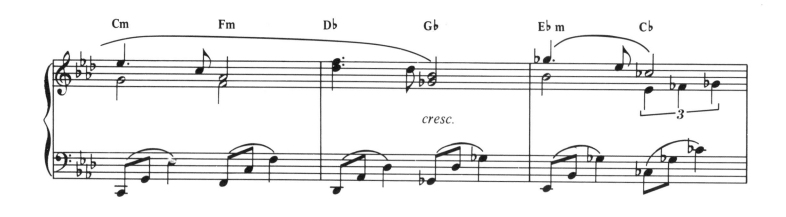

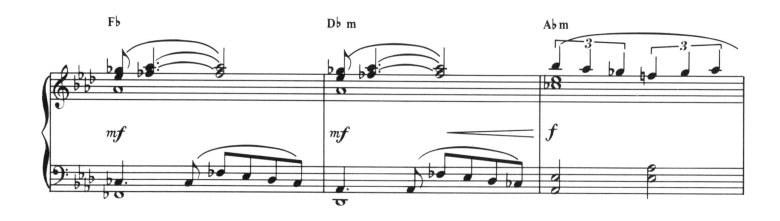

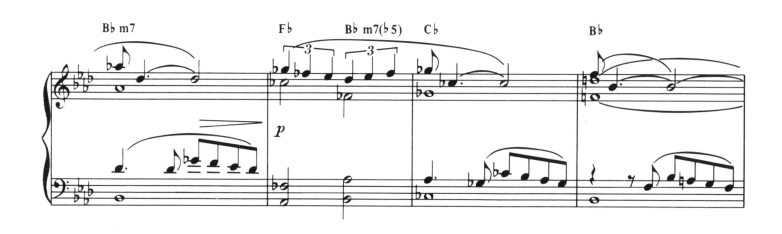

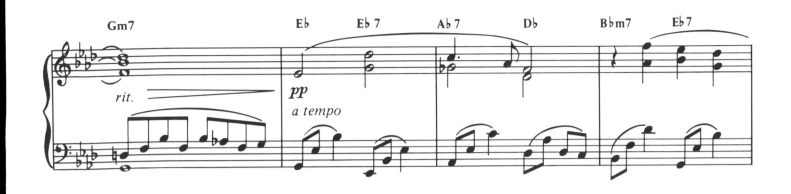

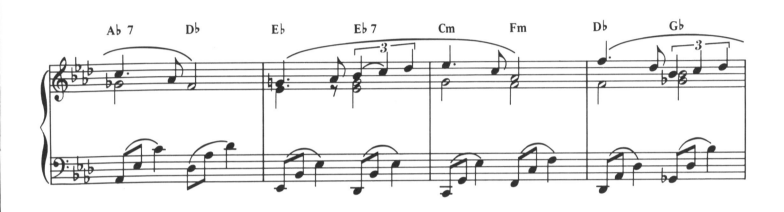

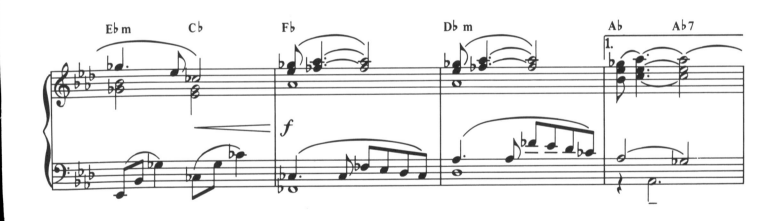

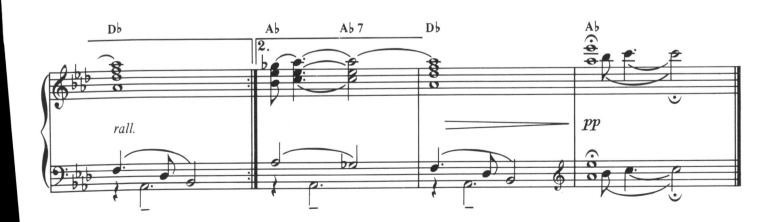

Willkommen
(from "Cabaret")

Words by Fred Ebb
Music by John Kander

Sunrise, Sunset
(from "Fiddler On The Roof")

Words by Sheldon Harnick
Music by Jerry Bock

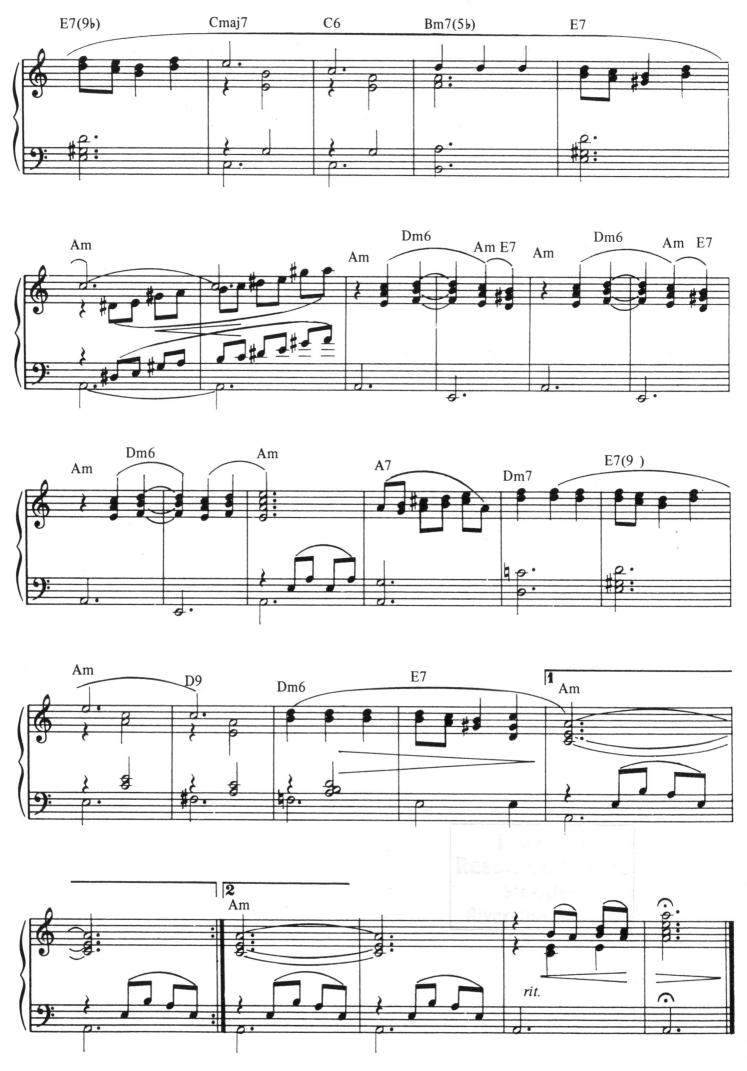

12/04 (53372)